# A Christmas to Share

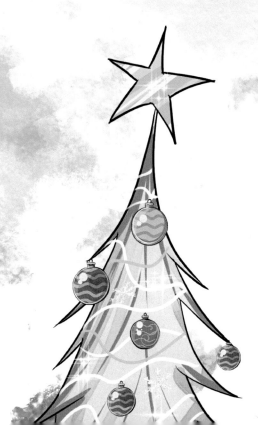

© 2024 Goodhearted Books Inc. (info@goodheartedbooks.com)
ISBN: 978-1-988779-75-1


Author          : Bachar Karroum
                  (In collaboration with Benoit Chalifoux)
Illustration    : Luis Peres
Graphic Design  : Samuel Gabriel
Proofreading    : Christine Campbell


Legal Deposit: Bibliothèque et Archives nationales du Québec, 2024.
Legal Deposit: Library and Archives Canada, 2024.

# A Christmas to Share

This book is the first in a long series titled "The Power of Kindness."

The goal of this series is to plant the seeds of kindness by inspiring children to see every situation as an opportunity to do good.

Kofi, the main character of this series, steps into various situations to bring a message of compassion and kindness. Originally from Africa, Kofi was born in Canada and lives with his mother in Quebec.

In this story, Kofi meets a new friend, Aïcha, who has just arrived from Morocco. When he senses Aïcha's interest in discovering Christmas, he doesn't hesitate for a moment to join her on this adventure.

Will he succeed in helping her discover the magic of Christmas? That's what we'll find out in the pages of this book.

November 15th... A special date for Aïcha and her family. The seven-year-old girl feels both anxious and excited. Yesterday, with a heavy heart, she said goodbye to her friends.

NOVEMBER

15

Today, at the airport, standing beside her mother, Fatima, she waves one last time to her father, who will join them later.

Canada awaits them.

On the plane, Aïcha watches the palm trees fade away through the window. Her reflection shows the tears streaming down her cheeks.

Exhausted by the emotions, she finally falls asleep.

The awakening is sudden. The landing is in 15 minutes. Aïcha opens her eyes, amazed by the magnificent landscapes of Montreal.

As soon as they land, everything speeds up. Aïcha and her mother take a bus to Donnacona. It's a quiet little town near Quebec City.

Next to them, a mother talks about Christmas with her daughter: the tree, the gifts, the decorations, and Christmas Eve!

Aïcha listens closely, curious.

On the way to their apartment, Aïcha admires the Christmas lights.

After hours of traveling, they finally arrive. Everything is new, different, and fascinating.

Aïcha is still a little sad. She thinks of her beautiful room in Morocco. Fatima holds her gently in her arms to comfort her.

At the table, Aïcha softly asks, "Can we celebrate Christmas this year?"

Fatima, worried, replies, "We'll see, sweetie."

On her first day of school, Aïcha feels lonely until a boy comes over.

"Hi, I'm Kofi. Do you want to play with us?"

Aïcha gladly agrees.

While playing, they talk about Christmas. "Do you celebrate Christmas in Morocco?" a child asks her.

"No, we celebrate Eid. We visit family and receive money gifts," Aïcha responds.

Curious, she adds, "And what's Christmas like?"

Kofi smiles. "It's a bit different, but just as special—you'll see!"

On the weekend, Aïcha and her mother go to the mall. The festive atmosphere amazes Aïcha. While standing in line to meet Santa, they run into Kofi and his mom Ama.

"Are you here to see Santa?" Kofi asks.

Aïcha smiles and says, "yesss!" but she looks at her mom, uncertain. Ama notices how fascinated Aïcha seems by Christmas.

Before falling asleep, Kofi and his mother read a Christmas story.
Kofi asks, "Why do we love Christmas so much, Mom?"

His mother smiles. "Because it's a time to celebrate
the birth of Jesus, a moment that reminds us to open
our hearts and share love and joy."

Inspired, Kofi suggests, "What if
we invited Aïcha and her mom?"

His mother, touched
by his kindness,
gladly agrees.

Today, the snow is falling like cotton. Aïcha and her mother walk slowly to school to enjoy the moment.

On the way, they meet Kofi and his mom. As they chat, Ama suggests, "Would you like to celebrate Christmas with us?"

Fatima, moved, promises to think about it. She hesitates between her traditions and her daughter's curiosity to discover new customs.

At home, they decorate the tree together.

Kofi adds garlands, and Aïcha places her decorations.

Their colorful tree sparkles with the joy of their friendship.

Fatima prepares a tagine while Ama cooks a tourtière. "These dishes go so well together!" Fatima says with a smile.

Meanwhile, Aïcha and Kofi decorate cookies.

After enjoying the meal, they end the evening with a Christmas movie.

Aïcha can't wait to return for Christmas Eve!

On December 24th, back at Kofi's house, Aïcha excitedly wraps a gift from Morocco for her friend.

The presents are nicely placed under the tree.

During dinner, a beautiful red cardinal appears at the window. Kofi's mother smiles, tears in her eyes. "That bird is a sign that your dad is watching over you, Kofi," she tells him.

"Merry Christmas, Dad," Kofi whispers, looking up at the sky.

"Dad, you're going to love Christmas," Aïcha adds, thinking of her father, who stayed in Morocco.

After the meal, Kofi's mother insists they stay over for the night. The children, excited, prepare for Santa's visit: carrots, cookies, milk, and stockings.

Aïcha adds dates from Morocco.

Tired, she finally falls asleep ...

On the morning of December 25th, Kofi and Aïcha run to the tree.

The dates are gone, a cookie is bitten, and the presents shine under the tree.

After opening them, Kofi hands Aïcha a package. "Here, this is for you."

She discovers a star-shaped pendant.

"It's a symbol of friendship; I received it from my dad before he went to heaven," Kofi says.

"Thank you, Kofi, it's beautiful," Aïcha says, moved by the gift.

It's time to leave. Aïcha and Fatima warmly thank Kofi and Ama.
Before stepping out the door, Aïcha turns around.
"Next year, it will be your turn to celebrate Eid with us!
My dad will be here."

"We would be honored to
share that celebration with
you," Ama says.

"With great pleasure!"
Kofi smiles.

Aïcha already feels at home, between her roots and her new traditions.

Fatima, watching her daughter, understands that what matters most is the kindness that unites hearts, far beyond borders and celebrations.

Made in the USA
Las Vegas, NV
21 November 2024

12302438R20019